DATE DUE

OCT 24 2013			
			PRINTED IN U.S.A.

Countries Around the World
England

Claire Throp

Heinemann Library
Chicago, Illinois

www.heinemannraintree.com
Visit our website to find out more information about Heinemann-Raintree books.

To order:
☎ Phone 888-454-2279
💻 Visit www.heinemannraintree.com to browse our catalog and order online.

Edited by Louise Galpine, Kate DeVilliers, and Laura Knowles
Designed by Richard Parker
Original illustrations © Capstone Global Library Ltd 2011
Illustrated by Oxford Designers & Illustrators
Picture research by Liz Alexander
Originated by Capstone Global Library Ltd
Printed in China by CTPS

15 14 13 12 11
10 9 8 7 6 5 4 3 2 1

Library of Congress Cataloging-in-Publication Data
Throp, Claire.
  England / Claire Throp.
    p. cm.—(Countries around the world)
  Includes bibliographical references and index.
  ISBN 978-1-4329-5201-3 (hc.)—ISBN 978-1-4329-5226-6 (pbk.)
1. England—Juvenile literature. I. Title.
  DA27.5.T57 2011
  942—dc22   2010044767

Acknowledgments
We would like to thank the following for permission to reproduce photographs: Alamy pp. 6 (© Mary Evans Picture Library), 11 (© North Wind Picture Archives), 32 (© Chris Wood), 35 (© Richard Peel); Corbis pp. 8 (© Nik Wheeler), 12 (© Hulton-Deutsch Collection), 24 (© David Leahy/cultura), 33 (© Toby Melville/Reuters); Getty Images pp. 21 (Daniel Berehulak), 30 (AFP), 39 (Dorling Kindersley); iStockphoto p. 37 (© Martin Lovatt); Photolibrary p. 27 (Monkey Business Images Ltd); Shutterstock pp. 5 (© Steve Smith), 7 (© Dmitry Chernobrov), 15 (© Richard Bowden), 16 (© Joop Snijder jr), 19 (© Paul Gibbings), 18 (© Rafal Olkis), 23 (© r.nagy), 25 (© Lara65), 28 (© Edyta Pawlowska), 29 (© Monkey Business Images), 31 (© Andry Alamsyah), 46 (© Gary Blakeley).

Cover photograph of two deck chairs on the beach at Brighton, with the Palace Pier in the background, reproduced with permission of Alamy/© M J Perris.

We would like to thank Rob Bowden for his invaluable help in the preparation of this book.

Every effort has been made to contact copyright holders of material reproduced in this book. Any omissions will be rectified in subsequent printings if notice is given to the publisher.

Disclaimer
All the Internet addresses (URLs) given in this book were valid at the time of going to press. However, due to the dynamic nature of the Internet, some addresses may have changed, or sites may have changed or ceased to exist since publication. While the author and publisher regret any inconvenience this may cause readers, no responsibility for any such changes can be accepted by either the author or the publisher.

Contents

Some words are printed in bold, **like this**. You can find out what they mean by looking in the glossary.

Introducing England

What comes to mind when you think about England? Historic buildings? Green fields? Fish and chips? Cricket? Wimbledon? England is known for all these things and more.

England or Britain?

There is often confusion about the difference between England, Great Britain, and the United Kingdom (UK). England is part of an island that includes Scotland and Wales, as well as many smaller islands around the coast. These countries make up Great Britain. The UK includes Northern Ireland, too.

Invasion by many forces over the years has led to a mixture of **cultures** and characteristics. This has particularly affected the English language, although most common words come from the Anglo-Saxon period.

My word!

Where do English words come from?

street	straet	(Romans)
rose	rosa	(Romans)
passport	passeport	(French)
landscape	landschap	(Dutch)

Saint George

Saint George is England's patron saint, and his feast day is celebrated on April 23. King Edward III made him a saint in the mid-1300s. Saint George is famous for slaying a dragon, but this is probably just a story. All we do know is that he was a Christian soldier, killed in the early 300s. It is also thought that he never actually set foot in England!

Small but attractive

England is a small country—about the size of the state of New York or Louisiana—but it attracts millions of visitors every year. People come to see unspoiled countryside, and experience culture in the form of art, theater, and music. England's great history also draws people to the country.

Many people visit North Yorkshire to go walking and take in the beautiful scenery.

History: Invasion and Empire

There is evidence that people lived in England 700,000 years ago. Stone tools have been found in Suffolk. England was later invaded by people from central Europe—the Celts—and by about 500 BCE, around 20 **tribes** lived in England.

The Romans

The Romans successfully invaded England in 43 CE under Emperor Claudius. They were soon in control of an area that included most of England and Wales, which they called Britannia. The Romans were responsible for bringing stability and wealth to England. In 313 CE they introduced **Christianity**. The Romans also left England with baths and a system of roads, among other things. They left around 410 CE.

BOUDICCA

Boudicca was the queen of the Iceni, a tribe that lived in the area around Norfolk and Suffolk. She is famous for very nearly defeating the Romans in England around 60 CE. Boudicca and her army got as far as Londinium (London), and killed many Roman soldiers, but the Romans crushed them in the end.

Boudicea, Queen of the Iceni.

Hadrian's Wall was built to separate England and Scotland, and was created in Roman times. It is named after Emperor Hadrian.

Viking invasion

Another invasion followed in 865 CE, this time by the Vikings. They came mainly from Denmark and conquered the east and northeast of England. Their capital city was Jorvik, which is now called York. They moved south and came up against Alfred, the king of Wessex. He is famous for pushing the Vikings back to the north. Alfred saved the English language by using it to **unite** the tribes he ruled over. He did this by using English to educate his people.

Perhaps the best-remembered date in English history is 1066. It is the date of the Battle of Hastings. William of Normandy (from France) fought King Harold for the crown of England, and won. The Bayeux Tapestry tells what happened during the Norman invasion.

A new church

Henry VIII is famous as the king who had six wives. While married to Catherine of Aragon, Henry fell in love with Anne Boleyn. Henry asked the **pope**, the leader of the Roman Catholic religion, to end his marriage with Catherine. The pope refused, so Henry created a new church, the Church of England, with himself as the head. He was then able to end his own marriage.

QUEEN ELIZABETH I (1533–1603)

Elizabeth I, daughter of Henry VIII and Anne Boleyn, came to the throne when she was 25, and ruled for 45 years. During this time England became rich and powerful, and the period is known as the Golden Age. Elizabeth famously never married and declared, "I have already joined myself in marriage to a husband, namely the kingdom of England."

English Civil War (1642–1649)

The Civil War was between the Royalists (or Cavaliers) and Oliver Cromwell's army, the Parliamentarians (or Roundheads). Many people thought King Charles I had too much power, and Parliament wanted more for themselves. The Parliamentarians won the war, and England became a **republic** under Cromwell's leadership. Cromwell's son took over after Oliver's death, but it was not long before Parliament asked Charles I's son to become King Charles II. However, Parliament now had far more control.

Great Britain

In 1536 the Act of Union joined England and Wales. In 1707 an Act of Union also joined Scotland to England, and the three countries became Great Britain. They were ruled by one parliament, based in London.

Daily life

In 1665 the **Great Plague** killed nearly one-fifth of the population of London. The plague spread to other places, such as Eyam in the north of England. The village closed itself off so that the disease could not spread farther. Food was left outside the village for the villagers inside to collect. They even had to dig their own graves.

American independence

The American Revolution (1775–1783) was fought between Great Britain and the thirteen North American colonies, which Great Britain ruled at the time. The colonies no longer wanted to be under British control. The colonies eventually won the war and became the United States of America.

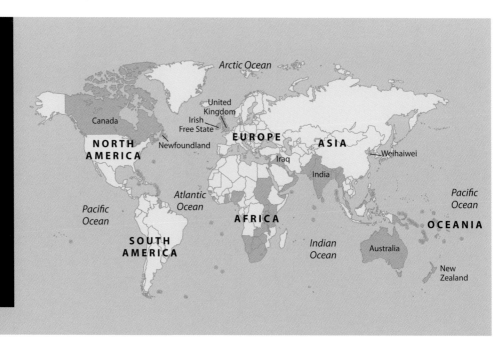

The British Empire was the largest empire the world had ever seen. At its height, it covered about a quarter of the world's land area, shown here in pink.

The Industrial Revolution saw factories, like this steel factory in Sheffield, built throughout England.

The Industrial Revolution

The **Industrial Revolution** was well under way when Queen Victoria came to the throne in 1837. New machines, such as the spinning jenny for spinning cotton, were invented that manufactured products quickly and in large numbers. Transportation improved, and trains carrying raw materials and goods ran the length of the country. England changed from a country mainly based on farming to one based on manufacturing.

Queen Victoria died in 1901. She had reigned longer than any other monarch. The expansion of the **British Empire** came to an end with her death.

Two World Wars

About one million Britons died in World War I (1914–1918), mainly while fighting in Belgium and France. However, in World War II (1939–1945) England was bombed by the Germans. London was badly affected. Thousands of children were evacuated (moved out) to live with families in **rural** areas. Prime Minister Winston Churchill became a national hero, inspiring the British to fight the Germans.

Daily life

During World War II, families had to survive on **rations** because the Germans prevented food ships from reaching Great Britain. People took ration books to stores and got a set amount of food in return for stamps. Potato Pete and Dr. Carrot were cartoon characters that encouraged people to grow their own vegetables.

During World War II, shopkeepers were only supplied with enough food for the people who registered with them.

After the war

Great Britain's economy suffered after World War II. The country had borrowed money from the United States to help pay for the war, but then struggled to pay it back. Britain was in a weakened state and was unable to stop many countries within the British Empire from gaining independence by the 1960s. In 1973 the United Kingdom joined the European Economic Community, now known as the **European Union (EU)**.

Margaret Thatcher, the leader of the Conservative party, became Britain's first woman prime minister in 1979. She led the country until 1990. In 1997, the Labor Party won the election, and Tony Blair became prime minister.

21st-century England

The global financial crisis that began in 2008 brought Britain into a **recession**. The **economy** slowed, with people losing their jobs and unable to spend as much money as before. The general election of 2010 was very close. The Labor Party had been in power, but a new government was formed, led by the Conservative party with Liberal Democrat party support.

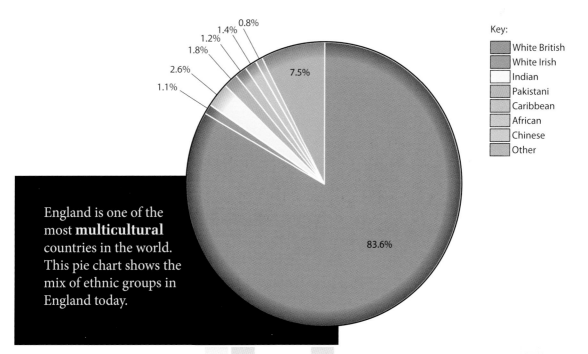

Key:
- White British
- White Irish
- Indian
- Pakistani
- Caribbean
- African
- Chinese
- Other

0.8%
1.4%
1.2%
1.8%
2.6%
1.1%
7.5%
83.6%

England is one of the most **multicultural** countries in the world. This pie chart shows the mix of ethnic groups in England today.

Regions and Resources: A Varied Landscape

England is one of three countries on one island. Scotland is to the north of England, and Wales is to the west. No place in England is far from the sea—the farthest is 77 miles (125 kilometers) from the coast. The seas that surround England are the North Sea, Irish Sea, and Atlantic Ocean. The English Channel is to the south and separates England from mainland Europe. At its narrowest point, France is just 21 miles (34 kilometers) away.

England is divided into 9 regions and 45 counties. The number of counties has changed over the years. For example, Yorkshire, a traditional county, was split into four in 1974.

This map shows some of the main natural features of England.

SCOTLAND

Cheviot Hills

Newcastle

Cumbrian Mountains

PENNINES

Scafell Pike

York

Manchester

Trent

ENGLAND

The Fens

Severn

Birmingham

Ouse

WALES

London

Bristol

Thames

N

Land height above sea level:

- Over 1000 kilometers
- Over 500 meters
- 200–500 meters
- Below 200 meters
- —— Country borders

0   160 kilometers

0   50   100 miles

Climate

English people are well known for talking about the weather. This is because it changes so quickly. One of the reasons for this is that England is part of an island. English summers are usually cooler than in Europe, but winters are normally milder. It is overcast on more than half the days of the year.

Landscape

The landscape in England varies from rolling hills, waterfalls, rivers, and lakes to the flat marshlands of the Fens and the Cumbrian Mountains. However, there are no real extremes. For example, Scafell Pike in the Lake District is the highest mountain at only 3,208 feet (978 meters).

This bar chart shows the average rainfall and maximum and minimum temperatures in England throughout the year.

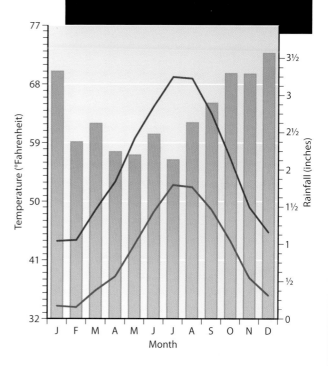

The Fens have been affected by climate change. It is thought that one million acres of land may be lost under water by 2030.

The coastline of England is about 5,581 miles (8,982 kilometers) long. The longest continuous stretch of it, and some of the most beautiful parts, are in Cornwall.

Rivers and mountains

The Thames is the longest river in England at 210 miles (338 kilometers). It begins near Cirencester in the west and travels as far as the North Sea. The Pennines mountain range is often called "the backbone of England," as it runs down the middle of the country, separating the northeast and the northwest.

Resources and trade

Coal and salt are among England's main **resources**. Sand, gravel, and clay provide raw materials for the construction industry. The United Kingdom's main **trade** is with Europe and the United States.

Jobs

In England there has been a shift from traditional industries, such as farming, and heavy industries, such as shipbuilding, toward services, such as finance or restaurants. However, cattle and sheep are farmed for the meat and milk they provide, and farms produce wheat, barley, and vegetables. About one-fifth of English workers have manufacturing jobs, such as food processing, textiles, and car making. Finance is a big part of the English economy. London is a major world center for banking and finance, but other cities, including Manchester, are also important. Tourism in England provides a lot of jobs in hotels and restaurants in tourist areas.

Economy

The 2008 global financial crisis affected the United Kingdom particularly badly. The economy slowed down. Unemployment rose to its highest since 1994. **Debt** was a huge problem, and the new government began working to reduce it immediately. Government debt had reached very high levels.

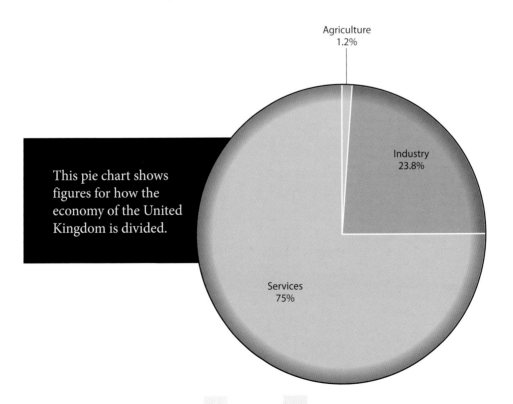

Agriculture
1.2%

Industry
23.8%

This pie chart shows figures for how the economy of the United Kingdom is divided.

Services
75%

Wildlife: Natural England

While much of England's landscape has been changed by people, there are still many areas where nature thrives.

Birds

The Royal Society for the Protection of Birds (RSPB) works for the protection of birds and wildlife and has over a million members. It's the biggest **conservation** charity in Europe. Birds that are common in England include English robins and blackbirds.

Animals

There are few **species** of amphibian or reptile in England. The adder, the only poisonous snake, is rare. Common animals include mammals, such as rabbits, gray squirrels, and foxes. **Endangered** animals include the water vole and the red squirrel.

It is thought that hedgehogs may be extinct in the UK by 2025. This is partly due to the loss of their natural **habitat**.

The New Forest National Park in southern England is the only part of the country that has hardly changed since Norman times. William the Conqueror made it a royal hunting preserve in 1079, so the land could not be built on. The New Forest is famous for its wild ponies.

National Parks

National Parks are areas protected for their natural beauty and wildlife. In England they are often privately owned, but are free and open to the public. Unlike national parks in some other countries, which are wilderness areas, in England they often include roads and villages. There are ten National Parks in England, including the Lake District in the north, which is famous for its lakes. Dartmoor has the largest open space in southern England, surrounded by rocky land and valleys. The Norfolk and Suffolk Broads are also usually included in the list of National Parks, although they were created separately. These protected areas cover about eight percent of England.

Reduced wildlife areas

England is a small country with a large population, so wildlife habitats are often under threat and sometimes destroyed. Destruction of **hedgerows** has meant that some birds, such as skylarks, have become rare in the countryside. Environmental pollution, such as chemicals used by farmers, and the introduction of species from other countries, has also affected England's wildlife.

As people have become more aware of habitat loss, campaigns have tried to stop habitat destruction. The National Forest in central England is one example. Nearly 8 million trees have been planted, helping to provide new habitats for wildlife. Farmers have also been offered financial help to reduce the amount of chemicals that end up in rivers, and to protect hedgerows and leave borders around fields to encourage wildlife to come back.

YOUNG PEOPLE

Eco-Schools is an international program that helps schools to become more **eco-friendly**. Students run the program themselves. They look at how environmentally friendly their school is and then choose what they want to improve, such as litter, waste, or energy, and how they will do it. Awards are gained when a school successfully shows improvements.

Getting rid of waste

Much of England's garbage is buried in **landfill sites**. Environmental campaigners think these sites may be full by 2015. Local governments are encouraging people to recycle as much as possible, and a landfill **tax** is charged on every ton of waste. One of the other options is incineration (burning), but there are environmental problems with this, too. Unless trash is burned at a particular temperature, it can release dangerous poisons into the air.

An increasingly common natural disaster to affect England is flooding. In recent years heavy rain has destroyed people's homes in places such as Tewkesbury.

Infrastructure: Constitutional Monarchy

The United Kingdom is a constitutional monarchy. The **monarch** is the **head of state**, but has no real power. The prime minister is the head of government. Along with Parliament, he or she is responsible for running the country.

Parliament is made up of two houses: the **House of Commons** and the **House of Lords**. Parliamentary elections are held at least every five years. Everyone over the age of 18 is allowed to **vote** for a Member of Parliament (MP). Local government includes county councils, which deal with education and planning. District councils deal with matters such as waste collection and housing.

This map shows the 9 regions and 45 counties in England.

Key:
- North East
- North West
- Yorkshire and the Humber
- West Midlands
- East Midlands
- East of England
- South East
- South West
- London
- —— Country borders
- —— County borders

SCOTLAND

Northumberland
Tyne & Wear
Cumbria
Durham
Teesside
North Yorkshire
Lancashire
East Riding of Yorkshire
Greater Manchester
W. Yorkshire
N. Lincolnshire
Merseyside
S. Yorkshire
Nottinghamshire
Cheshire
Derbyshire
Lincolnshire
Staffordshire
Rutland
Shropshire
Leicestershire
Norfolk
W. Midlands
Northamptonshire
Warwickshire
Cambridgeshire
Hereford & Worcester
Bedfordshire
Suffolk
WALES
Buckinghamshire
Essex
Gloucestershire
Hertfordshire
Bristol
Oxfordshire
London
Wiltshire
Berkshire
Somerset
Surrey
Kent
Hampshire
Dorset
W. Sussex
E. Sussex
Devon
Cornwall
Isle of Wight

0   160 kilometers

0   50   100 miles

N

The Houses of Parliament are based at Westminster in London.

European Union and NATO

The United Kingdom has been a member of the **European Union (EU)** since 1973. However, the UK chose to keep pound sterling as the **currency** rather than changing to the euro, the EU's currency, as most other European countries did. The UK is also a member of NATO and the United Nations, which aims to bring peace to troubled areas of the world.

THE PANKHURSTS

Emmeline Pankhurst and her daughter Christabel led the fight to get British women the vote. At first Emmeline fought for women to be allowed to vote in local elections. Then, along with her daughters, she founded a group whose members became known as suffragettes. Their actions shocked Britain as they smashed windows, got arrested, and went on hunger strike. Women gained the vote in 1918, but only for those over 30 years old. It wasn't until 1928 that women's voting rights were the same as men's.

Health care

The National Health Service (NHS) was set up in 1948. It allows everyone living in England, no matter how rich or poor, to see a doctor or get hospital care free of charge. There are sometimes long waits for major treatment so some people, if they can afford it, pay for private treatment.

Nurses make up the largest group of NHS workers.

Media

The BBC is a public service broadcaster. This means that they must provide television and radio programs that appeal to many different people. The money to finance the BBC comes from a licence fee paid by everyone who owns a television. Commercial television channels, such as ITV, have to get as many viewers as possible. Their money comes from companies wishing to advertise their products during programs. More viewers mean more money from advertisers, because their products will reach more people.

There are ten national newspapers in England as well as many local ones. The national papers range from tabloids, which include a lot of scandalous stories, to broadsheets, which are more serious.

Technology

In 2009, more than 18 million homes in the United Kingdom had access to the Internet. About 90 percent of those had **broadband**. **Rural** areas have more difficulty getting Internet access and mobile phone signals.

YOUNG PEOPLE

In a recent poll, it was found that 79.1 percent of children between ages 7 and 11 own their own cell phone, but only 72.7 percent own their own books. Many people worry that children's reading skills will only worsen as they spend more time on their phones. What do you think?

Many children in England spend a lot of time talking or texting on their cell phones!

School life

School in England is free, and children must go to school between the ages of five and sixteen. Many children also go to nursery school from the age of three. Some children go to private schools. All schools teach the same subjects as part of the **National Curriculum**. Subjects are taught at the same level in all schools.

The school year is usually divided into three terms, from the beginning of September until the end of July. This means that school vacations, or holidays, are at Christmas, Easter, and for six weeks during the summer.

YOUNG PEOPLE

School is from Monday to Friday only, unlike some countries where children have to go to school on Saturday. The school day usually lasts from around 9 a.m. until about 3:30 p.m. Most children stay in school for lunch, either buying a hot meal or bringing a packed lunch.

Elementary school

In elementary school children have classes on reading and writing, math, religious education, art, music, and physical education (PE). They also study simple science, history, and geography, as well as personal and social skills.

Most children in England have to wear a school uniform.

High school

At the age of 11 children go to high school. Students study a range of subjects, including at least one foreign language. At the age of 14 they begin to study for **GCSE**s, which are important exams. Depending on their GCSE exam results, they can then go on to do **A-levels** or courses at college.

Universities

From the age of 18, young people can continue their education at a university. This usually involves studying a subject in detail. England has some of the oldest universities in the world, including Oxford and Cambridge.

Culture: Pubs, Proms, and Cheese-Rolling

England is not known for its great food, but traditional English meals can be a real treat. They include the Sunday roast, fish and chips, and desserts, such as apple pie. Tea and coffee are popular drinks. Most people in England buy their food from supermarkets. Butchers, grocers, and bakers are becoming less common as a result of this. Farmers' markets can still be found in some towns a couple of times a week.

Pubs

A typical English tradition is going to the pub for a pint of beer! Nowadays this may be accompanied by a live band or by sports—usually soccer—on a big screen. Many pubs have outdoor seating so that families can go for lunch together. Some pubs even have activities for children, such as a bouncy castle in the back yard.

The London Eye opened in 2000 and has 3.5 million visitors a year. From the London Eye you can see up to 25 miles (40 kilometers) in all directions.

Apple crumble recipe

Ask an adult to help you make this delicious dessert.

Ingredients

- 2 cups apples
- 1 cup all-purpose flour
- ¾ cup butter
- ½ cup brown sugar, and 4 tablespoons for the apples
- pinch of salt

What to do

1. Preheat oven to 350°F (180°C).
2. Sift flour and salt into a large bowl and add butter. Rub together until mixture is crumbly.
3. Mix in sugar.
4. Peel, core, and chop the apples.
5. Place the apples in a pan with a tablespoonful of water and 4 tablespoons of sugar. Cook over a low heat for 5 minutes.
6. Put the apples in an ovenproof dish and cover with the crumble mixture.
7. Place in the oven and bake for 20–30 minutes until golden.

My word!

Where do these food-related English words come from?

cake	kaka	(Old Norse—from the Vikings)
lemon	limon	(French)
kettle	cetel	(Roman)

Music

Many people enjoy pop and rock music festivals during the English summer. Glastonbury, Leeds, and Reading Festivals are the best known and attract top singers and bands. The Proms and the Bath International Music Festival are examples of **classical** music festivals held every year.

Flag-waving is a big part of the Proms!

YOUNG PEOPLE

English pop and rock acts are popular worldwide and have been since the Beatles and Rolling Stones in the 1960s and 70s. In the 1980s, bands such as Duran Duran and Culture Club took the United States by storm. Now days bands such as Radiohead and Coldplay are popular in the United States and across Europe.

Literature

England has a long tradition of great authors who have become popular around the world. William Shakespeare is one of the most famous, but Jane Austen, Charles Dickens, the Brontë sisters, Agatha Christie, and many others are also very well known.

Art

Two of the best-known English artists are J. M. W. Turner and John Constable. Constable's paintings were often of Dedham Vale near his home on the Essex-Suffolk border. The area is known today as "Constable country." Turner was famous for his landscape paintings and had one of his pictures shown in an art gallery when he was only 15! There are many art galleries across the country devoted to both traditional and modern art, including works by artists such as Tracey Emin and Damien Hirst.

Antony Gormley designed the *Angel of the North* sculpture that sits on top of a hill near Gateshead in the northeast. The angel is made of steel.

Movies

Going to see movies is a popular pastime in England for all ages. Many of the movies people see are made in the United States, but British-made movies can often be a big hit, such as *Slumdog Millionaire*. This film helped lead to a rise in popularity in the West of Bollywood films, made by Indian companies.

Sports

Soccer (called football outside the U.S.) is England's most popular sport, both for watching and playing, but other events attract big crowds, such as the tennis at Wimbledon and horse racing at Ascot. England usually performs well in water sports, such as rowing and sailing. The fact that England is part of an island probably helps, as there is plenty of water around!

Big crowds can always be expected at England soccer matches.

The England cricket team beat Australia in in the famous **Ashes** series in both 2009 (shown here) and 2011.

London 2012 Olympics

In 2012 London hosts the Olympics. Improvements have been made in London's transportation system. New stadiums and accommodations have been built for the millions of people who will arrive in London to work, take part in, or watch the Olympics.

National anthem

"God Save the Queen," which is actually the British national anthem, is often played at sporting events for the England team. In the **Commonwealth Games** the British nations compete separately, so a different song is used. For the 2010 Commonwealth Games the public was asked to vote for this song. They picked "Jerusalem," a song used to **inspire** the England cricket team in the Ashes series against Australia in 2005.

Religion

In 2001 about three-quarters of the English population said they were Christian. The next most common religion was Islam, followed by Hinduism. In a more recent poll, about 43 percent of 16- to 19-year-olds said they do not believe in God.

National holidays

England does not have many national holidays in comparison to other countries. Most are called bank holidays, because banks are closed on these days. They include May Bank Holiday and Summer Bank Holiday, and always fall on a Monday. Christmas and Easter are the only religious holidays.

Some other days are celebrated, such as Remembrance Day in November, when those who died in wars are remembered. Bonfire Night also takes place in November. People have huge bonfires and fireworks. A straw "guy" is burned on the bonfire because in 1605 a group of men, including Guy Fawkes, planned to blow up Parliament while the king was there. Fortunately, they didn't succeed!

Festivals and events

Other festivals and events include Notting Hill Carnival in London and maypole dancing, a tradition carried out on May Day, the first day of May. In York there is the Jorvik Viking Festival. The strange but fun cheese-rolling event takes place in Gloucestershire. A wheel of cheese is rolled down a steep hill and people chase after it. The winner gets to keep the cheese!

My word!

Most areas of England have their own special words, known as slang:

have a look	have a mooch	(city of Birmingham)
money	splosh	(city of Liverpool)
house	hoos	(city of Newcastle)

These people have dressed up to take part in scenes from history at the Jorvik Viking Festival in York.

England Today

England had no strong **national identity** for many years until recently. There is no national dress. At many events where a national anthem is performed, Britain's national anthem is played, and no one is even sure what the English anthem is! However, Scotland and Wales gained their own governments in 1999, which seems to have encouraged more of an English national identity.

Sports is an area that brings the country together, and England flags can be seen attached to cars and buildings during events such as the World Cup. England has four-fifths of the UK population, and most people live in the southeast of the country. Some of England's cities, such as London and Birmingham, are among the most multicultural places in the world.

Daily life

Many English people love nature and the countryside. Although over 80 percent live in towns or cities, many people enjoy going to the country for long walks or to see spectacular scenery on their weekends. Parks are popular places for families to visit for a picnic or a stroll.

England: a good place to visit

England has beautiful countryside, interesting weather, and friendly people. Tourists flock to England to see its historical sites and learn about its interesting past. One thing is certain: nowhere in England is far from a castle, national park, country house, or other historical building.

Brighton Pavilion is a royal palace that was built for Prince George (later King George IV) in the late 1700s. He had a wild lifestyle and loved fashionable things.

Fact File

Official language:	English
Capital city:	London
Bordering countries:	Wales and Scotland
Government:	constitutional monarchy
Population:	51,809,700 (in 2009)
Life expectancy at birth (UK):	76.5 years for men; 81.6 years for women; ranked 25th in the world
Religious majority:	Church of England
National symbols:	red rose (flower), oak (tree), three lions (sporting badge)
Area:	50,301 square miles (130,279 square kilometers)
Coastline:	5,581 miles (8,982 kilometers) long
Longest river:	Thames at 215 miles (346 kilometers) long
Biggest lake:	Lake Windermere at 10 square miles (16 square kilometers)
Highest single-drop waterfall:	Hardraw Force, North Yorkshire
National Parks:	Lake District, Peak District, Northumberland, North York Moors, Yorkshire Dales, Dartmoor, Exmoor, New Forest, South Downs, and the Broads
Lowest point:	Holme Fen at 9 feet (2.75 meters) below sea level
Highest point:	Scafell Pike in the Lake District at 3,208 feet (978 meters)
Currency:	pound sterling
Natural resources:	coal, limestone, clay, gravel
Exports:	chemicals, food, drink
Imports:	food, fuel, machinery

Climate:	temperate
Public holidays:	8 bank holidays
Popularity as a tourist destination:	sixth in the world with 30.7 million visitors per year (2007, UK figures)
Festivals:	WOMAD (music), Glastonbury (music), Bath Festival of Children's Literature, Jorvik Viking Festival
Famous English people:	The Brontë sisters (authors), Agatha Christie (author), David Beckham (soccer player), John Lennon (musician), Diana Princess of Wales, Florence Nightingale (nurse), Charles Darwin (scientist), Margaret Thatcher (prime minister).

My word!

Some people from East London use Cockney rhyming slang when they talk. The slang uses words that rhyme with the word it actually means. Here are a few:

mate	*china plate*
beers	*Britney Spears*
stairs	*apples and pears*
easy	*lemon squeezy*
starving	*Lee Marvin*

England is famous for crafts such as the creation of china and porcelain pots and vases made by Wedgwood. Josiah Wedgwood, grandfather of Charles Darwin, started the company in 1759, and it's still going today.

Timeline

BCE is short for before the Common Era. BCE is added after a date and means that the date occurred before the birth of Jesus Christ, for example, 450 BCE.

CE is short for Common Era. CE is added after a date and means that the date occurred after the birth of Jesus Christ, for example, 720 CE.

700,000 years ago	Evidence shows that people were living in England at this time
around 3000 BCE	Stone Age people arrive from Iberian Peninsula
around 3000 BCE	Stonehenge is erected
55 BCE	Julius Caesar and the Roman army invade England
43 CE	The Roman army successfully invades England, under Emperor Claudius
around 60 CE	Roman army defeats Boudicca, queen of the Iceni
78–80 CE	Romans conquer southern England and Wales to form a new province called Britannia
410 CE	Romans withdraw from England
449–550 CE	England is separated into different kingdoms ruled by invaders, such as the Jutes, Angles, and Saxons
700s CE	Vikings from Denmark invade England
1066	William, Duke of Normandy wins the Battle of Hastings and conquers England
1348–1349	Nearly half the population is killed by a plague called the Black Death
1362	English is made the official language of Parliament
1534	King Henry VIII becomes head of the Church of England
1536	Act of Union joins England and Wales

1588	The Spanish Armada is defeated by Queen Elizabeth I's navy
1605	Guy Fawkes tries to blow up Parliament
1620	The Pilgrims sail for America
1707	Act of Union between England and Scotland
1775–1783	American Revolution takes place, resulting in the colonies becoming the United States of America
1700s	**Industrial Revolution** begins
1918	Women over age 30 get the vote
1914–1918	World War I
1939–1945	World War II
1979	Margaret Thatcher becomes United Kingdom's first woman prime minister
2005	Terrorist bombings in London
2008	Global financial crisis begins
2010	A General Election leads to the Conservative and Liberal Democrat parties forming a **coalition government**. The Prime Minister is David Cameron.

Glossary

A-levels stands for "advanced levels," which are entrance exams for UK public universities

Ashes series of cricket matches, played every two years, between England and Australia

British Empire group of countries that were ruled by Great Britain in the 1800s and early 1900s

broadband type of fast Internet connection

Christian related to the religion based on the teachings of Christ

classical serious, artistic music, often played by an orchestra or piano

coalition government temporary alliance between political parties. A coalition government happens when voting has been close and no party has been able to win a majority of the seats in Parliament.

Commonwealth Games games in which Commonwealth nations compete every four years. The Commonwealth includes countries that were part of the British Empire, such as New Zealand, Australia, and Canada. The games involve sports such as athletics, swimming, and boxing.

conservation protection of the environment

culture practices, traditions, and beliefs of a society

currency banknotes and coins accepted in exchange for goods and services

debt money owed to someone else

eco-friendly things that are helpful to the environment, such as recycling

economy to do with money and the industry and jobs in a country

endangered in danger of extinction

European Union (EU) political and economic union of (currently) 27 European countries

export sell goods to another country

Great Plague outbreak of disease in England in 1665. It spread easily from person to person, causing large swellings on the body. As many as 100,000 people may have died.

grocer shop that sells food

GCSE stands for "general certificate of secondary education" and is an examination in specific subjects for 16-year-old students

habitat environment in which a plant or animal is found

head of state main public representative of a country, such as a queen or president

hedgerow bushes planted in a row and usually used to separate fields

House of Commons first chamber of the law-making body of Parliament. The people choose the 650 Members of Parliament to sit in the House of Commons in a General Election. Each MP represents an area called a constituency.

House of Lords the second chamber of Parliament. Members are not elected but have been chosen by the queen on the recommendation of the prime minister.

import buy goods from another country

Industrial Revolution changes that took place in how goods were made, from small-scale production by people to large factories in which machines did most of the work. The Industrial Revolution began in the late 1700s in England.

inspire to affect with a particular feeling such as enthusiasm

landfill site place where garbage is buried underground

monarch king or queen who is head of state but has no real power

multicultural mix of people from different cultures and countries

National Curriculum plan of how subjects will be taught in all schools across England

national identity when people feel that they belong to a country and its culture and beliefs

pope leader of the Roman Catholic Church

ration fixed amount of food that someone is allowed

recession when economic activity slows, unemployment often rises, and interest rates fall over a period of time

republic country with an elected leader and no monarch

resource means available for a country to develop, such as minerals and energy sources

rural in the countryside

species type of animal or plant

tax money paid by people to the government. Taxes can come from wages or be placed on goods that people buy.

trade buying and selling of goods, usually between countries

tribe independent social group, historically often made up of primitive or nomadic people

unite bring together

vote to choose. People vote for someone to win an election.

Find Out More

Books

Allport, Alan, and George Wingfield. *England, 2nd edition*. New York: Chelsea House Publications, 2007.

Blashfield, Jean F. *England, revised edition*. Danbury, CT: Children's Press, 2006.

Boraas, Tracey. *England*. Mankato, MN: Capstone Press, 2006.

Bowden, Rob. *Settlements of the River Thames*. Chicago: Heinemann-Raintree, 2005.

Lister, Maree, Marti Sevier, and Roseline Ngcheong-Lum. *England*. New York: Benchmark Books, 2010.

Schemenauer, Elma. *Welcome to England*. North Mankato, MN: Child's World, 2008.

Simmons, Walter. *England*. Minneapolis: Bellwether Media, 2010.

Willingham, Elizabeth. *Teens in England*. Mankato, MN: Compass Point Books, 2008.

Websites

www.bbc.co.uk/history/historic_figures
This website has biographies of many of the people mentioned in this book. You can find out more about Boudicca, William Shakespeare, and Margaret Thatcher.

https://www.cia.gov/library/publications/the-world-factbook/geos/uk.html
The website of the CIA World Factbook is full of useful information about the United Kingdom.

www.eco-schools.org.uk
Learn about the Eco-schools program on this site.

www.nationalparks.gov.uk/learningabout.htm
Find out more about the UK's national parks on this government website.

Places to visit

If you ever get the chance to explore England, here are some of the places you could visit:

Arbeia Roman Fort and Museum
This fort on Hadrian's Wall in South Shields shows what life was like in Roman Britain.

British Museum
www.britishmuseum.org
This London museum contains ancient artifacts from Anglo-Saxon, Viking, and Roman Britain, as well as other amazing objects from around the world.

East Lancashire Railway
www.east-lancs-rly.co.uk
Have a ride on a steam train!

Jorvik Viking Center
www.jorvik-viking-centre.co.uk/about-jorvik
Visit this museum in York to learn more about the Vikings and how they invaded England.

Science Museum
www.sciencemuseum.org.uk
Visit the Science Museum in London to find out how science and technology have developed over the centuries.

Stonehenge
www.stonehenge.co.uk
Visit this ancient stone circle in Wiltshire and learn about how and why it may have been built.

Topic Tools

You can use these topic tools for your school projects. Trace the map onto a sheet of paper, using the thick black outline to guide you.

The flag of England is called the Saint George's Cross. It is known that the flag has been carried by soldiers in battle from the late 1100s, possibly earlier. Copy the flag design and then color in your picture. Make sure you use the right colors!

London ■

N

Index

Titles in the series